Curious George®
Home Run

Adaptation by Erica Zappy
Based on the TV series teleplay
written by Lazar Saric

Houghton Mifflin Harcourt Publishing Company
Boston   New York

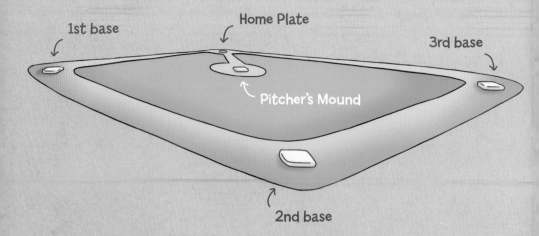

1st base

Home Plate

3rd base

Pitcher's Mound

2nd base

For information about permission to reproduce selections from this book, write to Permissions, Houghton Mifflin Harcourt Publishing Company, 215 Park Avenue South, New York, New York 10003.

Library of Congress Cataloging-in-Publication is on file.

ISBN: 978-0-547-69117-6 paper-over-board
ISBN: 978-0-547-69118-3 paperback
ISBN: 978-0-547-69122-0 paper-over-board bilingual
ISBN: 978-0-547-69114-5 paperback bilingual

Design by Anjali Pala

www.hmhbooks.com

Manufactured in China
SCP 10 9 8 7 6 5 4 3
4500424252

AGES	GRADES	GUIDED READING LEVEL	READING RECOVERY LEVEL	LEXILE ® LEVE
5–7	1-2	I	15-16	460L

Today George was going to his
first baseball game.
His friend Marco was playing.

Marco's team was the Cubby Bears.
They were playing the Tiger Babies.
Marco wanted to hit a home run.
He practiced batting.

Uh-oh.

The scorekeeper was sick.

"Will you help, George?" asked the coach.

Of course! George is always happy to help.

"Every time a team scores, you hang
a new number," said Marco.
That seemed easy!
But there were lots of numbers.

George waited and waited.
Sometimes baseball moves very slowly!
By the third inning, there were still no
numbers to hang.

Finally, there was some action!
Marco got a hit. His teammate got
one too! Marco slid into home plate
and scored one run.

Now George could put a number on the scoreboard. He pulled the number 5 out of the box and put it up.

"That's the wrong number!" said Marco.
George pulled another number from the
box. He put up the number 8.

"Use a lower number! You need to put the numbers up in order," said Marco. Order? What did that mean? George was curious.

Marco showed George how to put the
numbers in order.
"Like this: 1, 2, 3, 4, 5, 6, 7, 8, 9, and 10.
Now you try," said Marco.

George practiced putting the numbers
in order.
It worked! He kept score until the game
was tied at 4–4.

George heard a lot of noise
coming from the snack counter.
He could help hand out snacks.

George handed out the food order
for number 17.
Then 14.
"Wait," a customer said.
"The number 14 comes before 17!"
"Yeah! And 12 comes before 13!"
exclaimed another.

George was confused.
"Do you know your numbers?" the girl
at the snack bar asked.
He counted on his fingers from 1 to 10.

"Here's how to find out what comes after 10," she said. She held her hand over the 1 in the number 11 and the 1 in the number 12.

Now George knew that 11 comes
before 12, just like 1 comes before 2.
He gave the customers their snacks in
order.

When George returned to the game,
Marco was at bat.
But he had hurt his foot.
George would run the bases for Marco!

If Marco got three strikes,
he would get an out.
Strike one! Strike two!

Crack!
Marco hit
the ball hard!
George had to run *very* fast.

George made it around the bases! It was Marco's first home run. George was happy to change the scoreboard. The Cubby Bears had won 5–4!

Rules of the Game

Here are some basic baseball facts.

* **2** teams play against each other.
* There are always **9** players on the field:
    * A pitcher
    * A catcher
    * Players at first, second, and third base
    * Players in left field, right field, and centerfield
    * A shortstop
* There are **9 innings** in a baseball game.
* The winning team is the one that has scored the most runs at the end of nine innings.
* A team scores a run when a player crosses **home plate**.
* Each team has **3 outs** per inning.
* An out is made when
    * a batter gets **3 strikes** (a strike means the batter swung the bat but missed the ball!);
    * a player in the field catches a hit ball before it touches the ground;
    * or a player does not get to the next base before the ball does.

There are other ways to make an out, but these are the most common!

* There are **3 bases** on a baseball field, plus home plate.
* If a batter hits the ball and makes it to first base, that is called a **single**.
* If a batter hits the ball and makes it to second base, that is a **double**.
* When the batter hits the ball and makes it to third base after a hit, that is a **triple**.
* You might already know what happens if a player hits the ball far enough away (usually right out of the park!) to make it to home plate—that's a **home run!**

PLAY BALL!

Keeping Score

Next time you play a game with your friends or watch a baseball game on TV, try to keep score, just like George!

Materials:

- paper
- scissors
- a ruler
- tape
- colored pencils, markers, or crayons

Team A
2 0 3 4 1 1 2 1 2

Team B
1 2 1 1 2 1 0 1 2

Make your scorecards and scoreboard:

Before you begin, ask an adult for help.

1. Cut out twenty small paper rectangles.

2. Separate them into two piles of ten.

3. Using a colored pencil or marker, label one of the piles 1 through 10.

4. Repeat with the second pile, using a different color for the other team.

5. Use one large sheet of paper as your scoreboard. On the top left-hand side, write the one team name. Halfway down the paper on the left side, write the other team name.

6. Keep score by taping the card with the number of runs that each team has next to the name on the scoreboard.

7. Save the score cards and scoreboard and use them again!